THE POWER OF THE POSITIVE

11-2-12

The Power of the Positive

Live for Today!

Jason M. Taylor

BALBOA.
PRESS

A DIVISION OF HAY HOUSE

Balboa Press books may be ordered through booksellers or by contacting:

Balboa Press
A Division of Hay House
1663 Liberty Drive
Bloomington, IN 47403
www.balboapress.com
1-(877) 407-4847

Because of the dynamic nature of the Internet, any Web addresses or links contained in this book may have changed since publication and may no longer be valid. The views expressed in this work are solely those of the author and do not necessarily reflect the views of the publisher, and the publisher hereby disclaims any responsibility for them.

The author of this book does not dispense medical advice or prescribe the use of any technique as a form of treatment for physical, emotional, or medical problems without the advice of a physician, either directly or indirectly. The intent of the author is only to offer information of a general nature to help you in your quest for emotional and spiritual well-being. In the event you use any of the information in this book for yourself, which is your constitutional right, the author and the publisher assume no responsibility for your actions.

Any people depicted in stock imagery provided by Thinkstock are models, and such images are being used for illustrative purposes only. Certain stock imagery © Thinkstock.

ISBN: 978-1-4525-3185-4 (sc)
ISBN: 978-1-4525-3187-8 (dj)
ISBN: 978-1-4525-3186-1 (e)

Library of Congress Control Number: 2010919297

Printed in the United States of America

Balboa Press rev. date: 1/24/2011

DEDICATION

This book is dedicated to those who dream big, work hard, and rise up to explore the opportunities of today. It is also for those who uphold the ideals of success, goodwill, and a better world. Together, we can all do our part to drive improvement, promote happiness, and transcend greatness with *The Power of the Positive*.

In Memory

This book was written in loving memory of my late grandfather, William Arnold Taylor. He was a true gentleman who exuded class and honor in everything he ever did. He was also my best friend in life until he passed away in June 2001. He continues to be my inspiration, and I have committed myself to making him proud. Some may call it a coincidence that I finished writing this book on what would have been his eighty-ninth birthday, April 22, 2010. I simply call it destiny.

"Learn from yesterday; live for today; be better for tomorrow."

Contents

PREFACE

There is a different world out there—not the physical world we experience every day, but a psychological world where the meaning behind life's deepest intricacies are revealed. Unfortunately, this is a world some may never experience or be able to comprehend. Those who do understand this world and live it every day may find it difficult to realize that others simply do not. This different world I am referring to is the world of the positive, which is the basis for how I live my life. The positive world is about finding the good in everything and eliminating sources of negativity. Positive thoughts bring positive outcomes and the opportunity for a better life.

This mindset encompasses every aspect of life and is merely a different approach to the world we live in every day. In writing this book, I simply wanted to share my thoughts on life, which center around one essential ideal—the power of the positive. The power of the positive is about accomplishing great things and becoming empowered to do even more. Doing good things for yourself and others truly gives you more energy to dream bigger, work harder, and live better.

Unfortunately, we live in a world that focuses too much on the negatives and not nearly enough on the positives. It becomes easy to get caught up in all the negativity and accept this as the norm. However, when we simply take a different approach and see things with a positive, open mind, the world is an entirely different place. It is a place full of prosperity and opportunity.

Whether one chooses to pursue this type of mindset is an individual decision that everyone must make for himself. As I said before, some people may not be able to comprehend or embrace positivity, so keep in mind that this mindset is not for everyone. If you have an open mind, a desire to improve, and a drive to live life to the fullest, this book was written specifically for you. After reading this book, you too will be able to understand and embrace a state of mind you may never have thought existed.

The power of an individual can change a life, but the power of the positive can change the world.

FOUNDATION

B efore discussing the details of the positive world, it is important to explain the fundamentals, or building blocks, from which everything originates. Within this central ideal of positivity are three basic components that collectively create an opportunity for greatness and true happiness. Those components are learning, living, and loving.

I'll begin by explaining a personal life motto I developed that encompasses these basic fundamentals. It is this principle that I live by each day:

Learn from yesterday; live for today; be better for tomorrow.

First, learn from yesterday—pretty simple and yet so complex at the same time. Learning is all about improvement. It is about making a point to become better from each experience and taking something positive from every situation. It is also about taking time at the end of each day to look back on how the day went overall. Each night, while lying in bed, I quickly think back to all the experiences and interactions that were part of my day. I evaluate the things I did well and the things I want to improve on.

If we don't stop to learn from our pasts, we have no hope or potential of becoming better for the future. Self-reflection opens those pathways for improvement and personal development. It also allows individuals to find out who they really are and what they represent. The first step in self-improvement is learning from the past, and the second is about living in the present. This concept is the second piece of my life motto: "live for today."

Live for today. Ask yourself right now, are you living for today? I hope your answer is yes, in every sense of the word. No one knows how long the current lives we're living are going to last or whether or not we'll be given second chances. Therefore, it is so important to make the most of each and every day we have. That is what living for today is all about. So many individuals struggle with overcoming what's happened in the past and therefore miss out on the opportunities that today brings. As I mentioned previously, all we can do is learn from the past, not live in it.

The important point to note about the concept of living for today is that you must define for yourself what that truly means. We are all motivated by and enjoy a wide variety of different things. So, for example, if working on projects or enjoying time outside with friends and family is a way for me to live for today, that's great. However, if you do the things that make you happy and fulfilled, that's great too. This is what makes life so interesting—we are all unique individuals. Living for today means living your personal happiness—however you define it—every single day.

Another key to this concept is that it is dynamic in nature. By that, I mean living for today one day may be different from what it may be the next, since no single day is the same as any other. You may do certain things today that excite you, but yesterday was different and may have included other things that fulfilled you. Living is truly about focusing on today with the drive for a greater tomorrow. This leads me to explain the last piece of my life motto, "be better for tomorrow."

Be better for tomorrow—the final step of the process. Applying the same concept I discussed earlier about not living in the past, we can't allow ourselves to live in the future either. It becomes rather easy when times are tough to simply wish the next day, week, or year were here today. This is what wishing your life away is all about. Sure, we all have our share of bad days, but our reactions to those situations are what prepare us for the future. The struggles and joys we experience through life are what guide our development and fuel our drive to improve.

It's simply human nature to want to be better— just look at history and where we've come from; the examples are endless. We've desired means of traveling faster and thus developed automobiles and airplanes. Dreams of exploring outer space have been fulfilled by drive, dedication, and perseverance. Now, as we look to tomorrow, we too strive to solve the problems of future generations and to make this world a better place. It is this continuous drive to improve that makes humans so unique. The key is that we all must strive to improve as individuals so that we not only enjoy our personal successes, but reap the rewards of our collective efforts as well.

Learning and living become integral parts of our everyday lives, but perhaps the most important piece is what links it all together. This piece I am referring to is the third component in the foundation of a positive world—love. Love is all about emotion—it is the glue that unites our hearts and the spark that lights our souls. It is also about showing how much we care, showing the passion within, and allowing our feelings to guide us through our lives. Love can even be so strong at times that it generates conflict and hardship. However, love is everlasting, and no matter how far we waver off course, it always points us back down our paths of destiny.

The remainder of this book is about building on the foundation of learning, living, and loving in order to create the life you've always dreamed of. The most important thing to realize is that success and happiness are the direct results of a positive approach to these fundamentals. With an open mind and an open heart, the only limit to your personal potential is your wildest dreams.

I have always been intrigued by how the same fundamental principles apply to all aspects of life. Therefore, as you continue to read, keep in mind that nothing I discuss is specific to certain people or situations—it all truly applies to everything. It is also important to note that everything we do is directly related in some shape or form to business. Therefore, I occasionally illustrate key messages throughout the book with examples that show the similarities between running a successful business and running a successful life. If you think about it, your life is like your own personal business, and only you are the boss of your company. You determine what you want to include and the ultimate success and happiness of the life you live. If people thought of their lives this way, they would likely live them much differently.

Entrepreneurship is nothing more than an individual or group of individuals pursuing a successful career or business. Likewise, the world is nothing more than humans pursuing successful lives. Through personal experiences and those of others I've been able to learn from, I will show you what the power of the positive is all about and everything it represents.

Fully realizing the true potential of the power of the positive takes a certain set of tools or attributes. Whether developing a business, a career, or simply a lifestyle, we require proper tools. We were not born with all of them, but they can be developed through time. In fact, we were all born with unique characteristics and traits. It's simply a fact of life that we all have strengths and we all have weaknesses. However, we can overcome our weaknesses and further enhance our strengths to become more well-rounded individuals. After all, once we have the proper tools, the only limits to our potential are those we put on ourselves.

An individual who possesses or works to develop certain psychological traits can truly live a life much happier and more rewarding than most would ever consider possible. These traits are the tools we can then use to fulfill our ultimate goals in life. The key to understand is that these traits are psychological in nature, not physical. They have nothing to do with height, weight, strength, or any other external personal trait. This is something that most people, as well as the society we live in, have difficulty with. We as humans tend to be very superficial by conceiving thoughts, forming opinions, and making decisions based on physical traits. It is important to realize and embrace the fact that people are who they are because of their psychological make-ups, not their physical features. If individuals are truly at peace with themselves and how they live their lives, nothing else matters. This concept is very simple and fundamental to some, but it is so difficult and complex to others.

Now that I've introduced you to the concepts around the power of the positive, I will begin to share the details of how it all fits together. Keep in mind that the foundation of the power of the positive centers around learning, living, and loving. Throughout the remainder of this book, I will explain the traits I previously mentioned and how they relate to this ideal of a positive life. The first trait is allowing your mind to be free, open, and willing to dream.

DREAM

Impossibility made possible. Again, impossibility made possible. This is my definition of a dream in its purest form—so simple, yet so powerful. To break it down, I will start with "impossibility." Having a dream begins with focusing your heart on things you desire to become reality. Most dreams seem so farfetched and unachievable that many people choose not to pursue them. In the positive world, impossibility simply does not exist—if you can imagine it, you can make it happen.

To continue, the word "made." This is the action, the "do," the part that directly involves the dreamer. It is about doing whatever it takes to turn that dream into an experience. As a child, I used to dream about having my own home one day and making it everything I could possibly dream of. I imagined it would be large, with a beautiful view, and custom built to my specifications. At that time, I thought many of these ideas were too difficult and ambitious to actually achieve. However, over the last few years, I have been able to truly embrace this new mindset of positivity. In the process, I have been very focused and committed to doing everything it takes to turn my dreams into experiences.

The final word in my definition of a dream, "possible," is exactly what these experiences are. The "possible" is simply the reality, the result, or the real-life existence of the dream. To me, these experiences are what make life so rewarding. Some may doubt that a twenty-three-year-old would be able to have a job he truly enjoys, a beautiful new home, two cars, and a basement and deck he built with his own two hands. However, I did everything I needed and wanted to do in order to make those dreams come true. My dreams have fueled an inner drive and commitment to realize their existence. This is the power of the positive.

The key to understand is that these were personal dreams I set for myself. We all have dreams and goals that are unique to each of us. You have dreams that are important and special to you. We must be aware and respectful of the fact that people dream about and strive for a variety of different things in life. The integral component is focusing on your dreams so that you can reach your true potential and enjoy your ultimate happiness in life.

As we get older, we may allow ourselves to stop dreaming and our minds to become stagnant. Accepting your life today as "okay" or "it is what it is" hinders the possibilities of a better tomorrow. Instead, we must continue to challenge our minds, our hearts, and our dreams, since opportunities for a greater future are never ending. Young children are experts at dreaming big and allowing their hearts to run wild. They dream of becoming astronauts, doctors, firefighters, teachers, presidents, and more. Kids aren't focused on all the minor details that it takes to get them to their dream— just on the opportunity to fulfill that experience. Too often people think of dreams as visions you have as a child that will one day be fulfilled as an adult. This is definitely not the case; dreams can be for today, tomorrow, or any time to come down the road.

In addition, as we develop and become adults, we discover the complexities of our world. These complexities can become obstacles to our dreams and reaching our true potential. This is why taking a step back and reminding ourselves that the details will take care of themselves is so important. If we focus our efforts strictly on creating opportunities for our dreams to come true, the pieces will fall into place when the time is right.

As an adult, you should dream just as much as you did when you were a young child. Make a point to turn off your mind at times to allow your heart to show you the way to your hopes and dreams. I still have many dreams that I am working toward, and they are what motivate me each day. As I move forward into the future, I will continue to dream big and work hard so that I can later enjoy those dreams as reality.

As I mentioned before, entrepreneurship is nothing more than an individual or group of individuals pursuing a successful career or business. In many cases, these people are chasing dreams that may have started when they were children, while they were in school, or simply on a day when love ignited their souls. Without that initial dream of success and prosperity, the opportunity for living those experiences is never created.

Throughout this discussion of dreams and how important they are in guiding our futures, I have discussed some personal examples for illustration purposes only. However, it is up to you to evaluate where you stand with your dreams. Make a point of taking time out of your day to ensure you are moving closer to your goals in life.

There are truly no limits on what your dreams may be, and always remember that anything is possible. No matter the doubts or obstacles that may come your way, let your creativity and imagination be your guide to fulfilling your dreams.

In the same manner that dreams fuel our inner spirits, another trait within each of us does this as well. This leads me to explain the next trait, passion.

PASSION

A dream is the spark that ignites the fire of true passion, and love is the fuel that keeps the flame burning bright. Passion is nothing more than that special something that inspires us to work harder today for an even better tomorrow. It's what causes your heart to beat faster and your love to grow stronger. In order to find this spark, we must look inside ourselves and search for what drives us. The passion within each of us emanates from our hearts and extends through our souls. This raw emotion shows us our purposes and our paths in the journey of life.

In general, people are attracted to things that are "good" in life. We want to surround ourselves with the people and things that make us feel good inside. This inner happiness is the passion we all desire. Take a look at the world around you, and you'll notice that those who are truly passionate about what they do are both successful and fulfilled. Teachers who love to educate feel that passion when their students do well and show signs of growth and development. Stay-at-home moms are passionate about being there for those special moments that they will remember for a lifetime. Professionals driven by their careers want nothing more than even greater successes and a future at the top. Whatever your passion may be, embrace it, and don't allow society's opinions to cause you to question whether it's right. If it's right for you and you are happy, nothing else matters. The key to all of this is discovering that inner passion, and there truly is a way to find it.

I'd like to start by telling you how I found my true passion. I hope that discussing what it took for me will provide you with some insights on how you too can find your passion in life. I have learned a great deal through this process, so this is my opportunity to help you.

I have always dreamed of a future full of happiness and success. I dreamed of having a great family, close friends, and a fulfilling career. I've also always loved helping others, and now I have dreams and aspirations to help change the world in a positive way. These dreams include teaching everyone how to feel the prosperity and exhilaration of life. By shifting the focus of our world on the positive today, we will proceed in a new direction for a better tomorrow. Until recently, however, I have never quite known what it was that would make all of these dreams come true. I began to realize that there had to be a fork in my path of destiny.

It wasn't until I was living alone during my last years of college that my life began to change significantly. Instead of looking strictly at the world around me, I began to look at the one thing I have complete control of: myself. Up to that point, I filled my spare time with distractions—things like watching television, surfing the Internet, or playing computer games. Rather than distracting my mind, I decided to create an opportunity to listen to my heart. I searched deep within to find out who I was, the things I wanted to stand for, and who I truly wanted to be. In some cases, the principles I wanted to stand for didn't match the person I was at the time. It was this realization that inspired a commitment I made to myself. That commitment was to ensure that the values I wanted to stand for and the person I wanted to be matched exactly who I was. It was also to make a point every single day to do the things I wanted and needed to do to get me one step closer to my ultimate dreams. This process was uncomfortable at first, as I learned things about myself that I wasn't proud of. However, I was able to admit my imperfections and started focusing strictly on becoming a better person.

These components of my personal commitment encompass a concept I refer to as "living your priorities." This is another opportunity to ask yourself a question— do you live by your priorities? Sure, we all live our lives according to some sort of priority schedule that we've set for ourselves. However, the key is making sure your time and energy are allocated according to that priority schedule each and every day. In addition, it is important to ensure that the priorities you are living match those that you truly want to be living. As I began to look inside myself, I realized that I was spending too much time and energy on things that truly didn't matter. Furthermore, many of those things I had absolutely no control over. It was through this realization that I began to make a conscious effort to get myself back on track.

So, the first step was asking myself what my true priorities were in life. For example, feeling good inside, being a more positive person, getting good grades, and being able to get a great job after college were a few of mine at the time. The next step was aligning my daily activities with those priorities. I worked out, which made me feel better physically and psychologically. I made a point to smile and work on some of the qualities I wanted to improve, such as my patience and temper. These allowed me to become a more positive person. I also studied hard and actively pursued the companies that stood for the same values I did. These activities helped me to perform strong academically and obtain that great job I was searching for. When I looked back at the end of the day, I had literally lived my priorities. This was the final step—reflecting back to ensure the priorities I had set were exactly those that I was actually living. This process was integral to finding my true passion and changed the way I approached life. Again, take the time to answer the question—are you living your priorities each and every day?

In the same manner that I strove to live my priorities, I also made a point to live my morals and values. For the most part, I did, but there were times when I allowed my surroundings and others around me to alter or sway the values I stood for. My intentions may have been good, but my actions told a different story. I am a firm believer that actions speak louder than words. People can say anything, but it's their actions that show their true characters. I wanted to ensure that the principles I chose to stand for were the same as those that others saw in me. My personal interactions with them and the world around me would be the representation of those values. This is what setting personal expectations is all about.

Living both my priorities and my personal expectations laid the foundation for allowing my passion to come through. I made a point to act on the feelings of my heart instead of the thoughts of my mind. Up to that point, I constantly found myself suppressing my inner emotions and acted solely on what my mind was telling me to do. After all, it is your mind that tells you what you need to do, but it's your heart that tells you what you want to do. If that's difficult to understand, think of it this way—your mind will ensure you brush your teeth and tie your shoes, but your heart will be there to make sure you smile and tell your family you love them.

Throughout this process, I also started to understand and embrace that I was a good person and stood for strong values. I've seen that those I interact with each day respect and appreciate my values as well. The confidence I've acquired through this development has pushed me to want more and to want better.

After graduating college, I started my career as an engineer for a large global corporation and moved into my first new home. I've created a positive environment that allows me to be happy and enjoy everything that life has to offer. It's also allowed some of my wildest childhood dreams to come true. Through the initial success and happiness I've enjoyed, I've developed a desire to help others do the same. However, personal experiences and individuals in my life have shown me that some people struggle to see the positivity in our world. I've also seen that a large number of people want to be happy and want to find what they truly love, but they simply don't know how. I feel that I have the ability to show others all across the world how true happiness can be achieved. I feel this is a gift I've been given, and I am committed to making the most of this opportunity. I embrace an obligation to help change the world in a positive way through teaching others how to live their dreams. This is my true passion—the fuel that keeps me burning bright.

This time when I lived alone was the turning point in my life and a period I will never forget. It was the point when I finally stopped asking what the world could give to me and started asking what I could give to the world. After all, why should I assume that the world owes me something? Instead, what can I, as an individual, contribute to make this world a better place? The more we give, the more we get back. This was a concept I first learned about and found interesting as a child in elementary history class. In his 1961 presidential inaugural address, John F. Kennedy proclaimed, "Ask not what your country can do for you—ask what you can do for your country." Instead of merely finding it interesting,

I finally embraced this concept as something I wanted to live every day. Now I see each morning as a fresh start and a new opportunity for me to help make this world a better place. Can you imagine if we all could find our true passions and do our parts to help the world? If we all make a point of finding that personal inner passion and living it every day, we can collectively experience the rewards of our endeavors. I have no doubt that one day we will all discover and fulfill our true purposes in life. This is the power of the positive.

This turning point was that fork in the path I mentioned earlier, when I started in a new direction in pursuit of a better life. This was not something that happened by accident or luck. I removed the distractions from my life and took the time to get to know myself better than I ever had before. I focused my time and energy strictly on living my true priorities and finding my reason for being. This is exactly what inspired me to write this book and make spreading the message of positivity my career.

This is my story of finding my true passion. You have your story—it is special and unique to you as an individual. You may have already found your passions in life, or you may still be in search of them, and that's okay. Sometimes as we move through life, we grow, and our passions may change or new ones develop. In any case, if you're in pursuit of that spark that lights your soul, make a point of finding it and embrace it.

As you strive to become better, create a positive environment where you have an opportunity to search inside yourself and listen to the voice of your heart. Establish your personal expectations, values, and priorities. Ensure they represent everything you want to be and everything you want to stand for. Set them high and work hard to live up to them. Most importantly, live them in everything that you do and be proud of who you are. Always be strong and confident so that others' opinions, doubts, or actions don't alter your expectations, values, and priorities. The world around you will see through your actions, not your words, what you expect and stand for. Those who truly matter in your life will appreciate the high standards you've set and will be motivated to do the same so that they too can improve and live great lives.

If you are a parent, make sure your children would be proud of how you act and the principles you stand for. As they grow and develop, they too will learn to be good people. After all, your children are living examples of the values and morals you instilled in them. It is also important to realize that being a good parent isn't always about being a best friend. At times it won't be easy, and they won't understand why you're being tough, but as they grow older, they will realize and appreciate that you were always doing what was best for them. You will find great pride in leading by example and sending a positive message to those around you.

As you move forward, have confidence in your desire to improve, and relish your journey toward ultimate happiness. Refuse to accept life as a right; embrace it as a privilege and an opportunity. Fill your positive world with everything you dream it to be and everything your heart desires. You will then be able to find that inner passion that leads you down your path of destiny. Show the world why you're here, and leave a positive impression.

This journey of life is not a sprint; it is a marathon. Therefore, it is important to keep in mind that we all develop and progress at different paces. In addition, we also may find our passions at different stages in our lives, and that's okay. However, the key is realizing they're out there and understanding how to discover them.

As I went through this process, I learned that by turning off your mind and turning on your heart, your true passion shines through. As you free yourself from the day-to-day worries, doubts, and frustrations your mind emits, your soul awakens. It then begins to flourish as you immerse yourself in the joys of your life. Your mind takes a pause to listen to the voice of your heart. Creating such opportunities opens the pathways to uncovering your true purpose. Always remember, our minds will lead us through our days, but our hearts will lead us through our lives. It is an interesting concept, and one that proves true time and time again.

Since the turning point in my life originated with the decision to look inside myself, I want to further explain the importance of self-reflection. As I mentioned previously, self-reflection creates opportunities for personal development and improvement. This is the next trait I will discuss.

SELF-REFLECTION

Life is so short when you truly stop and think about it. Time seems to pass in an instant, leaving you wondering where it all went. Therefore, it is important to enjoy each and every minute of this amazing experience. Because of the fast-paced nature of the world we live in, we must always remember to take time to stop and reflect on where we are and where we want to go. Falling into a state of complacency becomes so easy with the numerous day-to-day responsibilities we all have. However, without taking a step back to see where things stand, how can we ever ensure that we, and the lives we live, are progressing on the tracks we intended?

I believe everyone has the potential to develop so deeply by simply prioritizing self-reflection. I have bad days just like everyone else and am not a perfect person. I do, however, take time to think about why I reacted to something the way I did or how I approached certain situations. As I mentioned previously, I make a point at the end of each day to reflect on how the day went overall. At times, I realize that I could possibly have done things differently, potentially resulting in a more positive outcome. It is through these realizations that we learn, grow, and develop as individuals.

Since developing a more open-minded approach to the world, I have seen others who find admitting their mistakes or instances when they were wrong very difficult. Some people feel that they simply can't be wrong and that their way of doing things is the best or only way. The root of this problem lies in one simple personality trait— ego. Letting go of your ego is imperative to making this process of self-reflection work. After all, egos are nothing more than exaggerated opinions of ourselves. They are walls that separate our subconscious minds from our hearts. These walls also hinder our ability to admit our mistakes and wrongdoings. They prevent us from doing what's right when our emotions tell us what's wrong.

The key to all of this is understanding that no one is perfect. We all have talents, and we all have faults. As a whole, we can learn from others to conquer our weaknesses and teach them through our strengths. Without removing the ego or stubbornness, this becomes extremely difficult. However, through self-reflection, this process becomes much easier. Asking for help when we're unsure or in need becomes simple and easy. We become comfortable with making mistakes and admitting our imperfections.

I have experienced firsthand the personal growth and development possible after committing oneself to these ideals. So, as you strive to become better, make a point to let go of your ego, and embrace the relief of no longer having that artificial expectation of perfection hanging over yourself. You'll truly find peace in accepting that you're human just like those around you.

By allowing yourself to be at ease with your strengths and weaknesses, you also develop an open-minded view of your surroundings. You begin to see yourself and the world around you as one united entity, full of potential and opportunity. Viewing the world as a puzzle, you become an integral piece and realize that you play a part in making it all come together. Through this process, you also begin to realize that your life is in your hands and that you determine everything you want it to be. As you embrace this new view of yourself in the world, you no longer see other people as reference points for measuring your success and happiness.

Self-reflection is merely a benchmarking process against yourself, not others. Too often we get so caught up in comparing ourselves to other people that we start to feel as if we have to do more or do things differently. However, by setting personal expectations and priorities, you establish benchmarking standards for yourself as an individual. As I've mentioned previously, we're all unique, and there's no one else out there exactly like you. Therefore, when evaluating where you stand with your personal goals and values, you can't compare yourself to other people. They are different and have no effect on how you choose to live your life. Others' opinions, beliefs, and expectations are sometimes quite different from your own. Therefore, it is critical to maintain your inner strength, overcome distractions, and stay focused on living your life. It's a big world out there with plenty of obstacles that can prevent you from reaching your dreams and aspirations. However, with the focus and confidence that you're doing the right thing, those obstacles become the hurdles that make you strive for even better.

This benchmarking process is applicable and beneficial in all facets of life. In the business world, managers often use appraisals as a metric to evaluate performance. This is another type of reflection process, but it differs in some ways from that of self-reflection. In many cases, individuals are evaluated based on personal performance in comparison with other employees within the organization. This occurs for good reason. In business, those who drive productivity and improvement take the company to the next level. These individuals are highly motivated and accept nothing less than success. Without stopping to take time and evaluate employees' progress, recognizing those well performing employees and what they've accomplished is nearly impossible.

Many businesses also spend a great deal of time, effort, and money on their employees' development. As individuals within the company expand their talents and abilities, the company as a whole thrives. This same template of development can be applied to a more macro-economic level. Employee growth leads to team and organizational growth. Organizational growth leads to industry growth. Industry growth leads to national economic growth. Finally, national growth leads to global economic growth. So, the world economy develops and strengthens, and the individual's growth is at the core of it all.

Self-reflection is simply taking a similar approach at the personal level in order to continuously improve. I discussed earlier the idea of your life being your personal business with you as the owner. If we can all grow and develop independently, we all improve and become better together. On a personal level, individual growth leads to family growth. Family growth leads to community growth. Community growth leads to state and national growth. Finally, national growth leads to the growth of the world. This is exactly how the world can evolve into a world our wildest dreams would struggle to imagine. This process of self-reflection is nothing more than creating that opportunity for you to become better. As you become better, so does the world around you. This is the power of the positive.

So what does this word "better" truly mean? The word "better" can have a variety of definitions, which you can create for yourself. Some people may wish to improve at a specific skill, sport, or trade. Others may see "better" as learning something totally new so that they can develop and expand their personal interests or abilities. "Better" is even more powerful in the internal context—where you become mentally stronger, more confident, or more aware psychologically. To put it simply, "better" is merely an improvement from what currently exists. As you strive to become better, create those definitions of the word for yourself and make time to learn and grow as an individual.

There are two integral components to the success of self-reflection. These components are the "where" and the "how" of the process. You know yourself better than anyone. You know how you learn best and the type of setting that allows you to do so.

Let's start by discussing the "where," the environment you establish to reflect and learn about yourself. Since we all learn differently, it's up to you to create the best conditions for you to grow and develop. If you are more of an individual learner, dedicate time to being alone to relieve your mind of life's distractions. Go to that special place that makes you feel comfortable and causes your soul to be free. On the other hand, if you learn better in groups, join others in your pursuit of happiness and learn with those around you. Whether this occurs through chat rooms, private meetings, or group discussions, all of these environments create a setting that allows for self-reflection and personal development.

Now let's discuss the "how," the manner in which you self-reflect. Some people learn through writing or reading, some through speaking, and others through listening. As I said before, you know how you learn best, so make the most of that approach. If you learn through writing, start a journal or daily log and spend time documenting the words of your heart. If reading is your inspirational connection to higher thinking, read books, articles, and other literature that sparks your interest. If talking with others allows you to learn best, allocate time to meet with those with whom you share common desires. Finally, if you learn best through listening, attend conferences, seminars, or speeches about the ideals you value and wish to learn more about.

The key to the "where" and "how" components is to ensure your mind is at ease and your heart is engaged. Your emotions and passions will shine through as you open yourself to self-reflection. You will begin to find your role and your reason for being.

The self-reflection process is another pivotal element to reaching true happiness and fulfillment in life. It takes you one step closer to realizing the true power of the positive. Self-reflection does take time, and you have to dedicate a portion of yours to it. It doesn't always have to take long; simply stopping what you're doing and thinking about what's happened is all it takes. However, the more time you dedicate, the more you'll learn about yourself and the world around you.

Through one simple process, two of the three pieces to my life motto are encompassed. As a reminder, that principle is: "Learn from yesterday; live for today; be better for tomorrow."

Self-reflection allows you to learn from your past to be better for your future. Dedicating time to look back and reflect on our past is an integral step in personal development, but it's also imperative that we look to the future. In order to create that opportunity for our hopes and dreams to become experiences, we must strongly believe they will exist when the time is right. This belief requires our imaginations to emerge and inspire our creativity. The guiding light to this inspiration is vision, the trait I will now discuss.

VISION

As you continue to progress through life, you will find that each day brings new adventures, challenges, and opportunities. Each day also brings times of happiness, loneliness, confusion, excitement, and a variety of other emotions that cause deep inner connections between our minds and hearts. Our emotions and feelings bring about unique connections to this world we live in. We connect with the people, places, and things that are parts of our everyday lives. The unifying link between our emotional selves and our surroundings is our senses. Our senses directly connect us to the world and everything it possesses. The way we approach, react, and respond to our lives involves engaging our senses and harnessing our emotions. Too often we suppress the feelings we perceive through our senses instead of acting upon the insights they provide us. At times we must also exude patience to fully embrace the true meaning of our emotions. This ultimately becomes a delicate balance that we must learn to manage.

One of our senses, vision, unites our wildest dreams with the belief that anything's possible. It is the vision within us all that, when used to its fullest potential, opens doors to life's greatest experiences. We are all born with inner vision, but it is up to each of us to develop it and use it to our personal advantage. It is important to note that some people do not have the natural aptitude to see the potential that exists in our world, and yet others display it with ease. This level of perception requires an open outlook, a sense of hope, and a strong sense of vision.

The vision I am referring to is not what people typically associate with the word. Vision is much deeper than simply painting a picture of the future. It is about embracing the idea that believing is seeing. This is an important concept, so allow me to further explain its meaning. Vision is the source of creativity, inspiration, and possibility in this world. In order to create an opportunity for our hopes and dreams to come true, we must first believe that they are possible. As you begin to put thoughts and beliefs out there, you will establish the potential for their existence in the universe. As I've mentioned before, if you can dream something and believe it's possible, it has the ability to become reality.

Vision is the first step because it establishes possibility. Then, the shift from possible to probable takes place when you begin to take action on those dreams. Finally, the transformation from probable to certain arises when you live and breathe everything it takes to make the dream happen. You become committed to living that initial vision as an amazing experience.

Unfortunately, many people take the opposite approach that seeing is believing. They believe you have to physically see something firsthand before you can believe it exists. The application of this philosophy restricts our true potential in life. If everything had to be demonstrated or proven to us, the accomplishments of those who came before us would have to cease to exist. Throughout the course of time, our dreams, imaginations, and creativity have inspired the innovations that have shaped the lives we live.

On a more fundamental level, vision is the ability to see and observe the happenings of today. As you discover the events that unfold and the people around you, examine their purpose. You can truly learn something from every situation and every individual who in some way affects your life. Make a point to keep an open eye and an open mind to the world. Even the blind, who are physically unable to see life taking place around them, possess this trait of vision. They rely on their imaginations to paint their pictures of the world. This psychological awareness of your surroundings is also important to your personal growth and development. Today's proceedings provide the lessons to prepare you for those that may come tomorrow. I use the word *may* instead of *will* because it is important to remember that tomorrow is never a guarantee. Live for today, and if you're given the gift of life tomorrow, opportunities will be there for you.

Vision is only one of the senses we've been given to absorb everything this world has to offer. We've also been given the ability to hear, touch, taste, and smell. These senses are the connecting links to experiencing life's most intricate characteristics. They are the tools and guides to uncovering our ultimate pleasures. As I mentioned previously, our senses are integral components to our perceptions, approaches, and reactions to our daily encounters. Through a profound understanding of their existence, we unlock the potential for discovery. I'd like to discuss each of these senses with greater depth and bring light to the value of developing a closer outlook on the world.

The sense of hearing is truly a gift, and it too is a trait that some never have the chance to experience. Cherish it, and use it to its fullest potential. Instead of always talking or entertaining your mind with distractions, listen to the world around you. Listen to understand others' views and expand your horizons through what you hear. In a deeper sense, listen to your voice within, your emotions, and your inner soul. I mentioned previously that your heart leads you through your life, so make a point of listening to what it has to say. As you do, you will begin to hear the passion, the excitement, and the love that emanate from within you.

Our sense of touch provides us with another form of contact with our environments. We shake hands to demonstrate our kindness, give hugs to show our love, and grasp firmly our most prized possessions. You have the power to put your personal touch on this amazing world we live in. Leave your mark of greatness, and allow others to benefit from the positive qualities and attributes you possess. Make a point each day to show your passion and enthusiasm toward everything you do. If we each make those personal contributions, we can collectively enjoy life's greatest gifts. You bring something totally unique, so share it with those around you. As Gandhi once said, "In a gentle way, you can shake the world."

Taste and smell allow us to indulge in the world's flavors and aromas. Nourish your body with the nutrients that will fuel your mind, spirit, and heart. A healthy soul promotes your drive and determination to reach your true potential. When your inner self is fulfilled, you begin to savor the success of your daily accomplishments. You simultaneously exude confidence and happiness for others to see. The phrase "stop and smell the roses" is something we all need to embrace as we proceed through life. Such an approach allows us to further enhance our connections with the environments we live in. Make a point throughout your days to do just that—soak up everything around you and the pleasures life provides.

In order to receive the offerings of the world, take a deep breath, enjoy the moment, and allow your senses to run wild. When you dream, be specific with your aspirations and engage your senses. Make a point to refine these senses to be more perceptive, attentive, and responsive. Appreciate things for their deeper meaning and everything they represent. As an example, refuse to see today as just another day and instead, view it as an opportunity to do something special. Absorb the beauty of the world around you, and cherish its greatness. When you find yourself getting off course in life, trust your senses to get you back on track. Let your surroundings help fuel your strength and desire to change this amazing place for the benefit of us all. This is the power of the positive.

One of the great aspects of life is that we cannot predict the future. However, we can envision a future that consists of all the positive things we hope and dream for. You can now embrace the idea that your thoughts are the drivers of your life. Your senses allow you to connect these thoughts with your deepest emotions. With vision and conviction behind your greatest ambitions, you create the opportunity for their existence. However, it takes enthusiasm, dedication, and perseverance to see your ambitions through. The foundation behind those driving attributes is confidence. With it, you can do anything, but without it, you become consumed by the obstacles of our world. I will now discuss the importance of confidence and its ability to help manifest your true potential.

CONFIDENCE

Success or failure, victory or defeat, happiness or disappointment—these are your options; what will you choose? You make these decisions on a daily basis, whether you realize it or not. If you accept nothing less than success, victory, and happiness in everything you do, you're on the right track. However, if you find yourself disappointed, defeated, and overcome by failure, here's your opportunity to change all that. Vision establishes the belief in possibility, but now it's time to make your dreams come true. Creating the opportunity to transform possibility to reality requires drive, commitment, and persistence. The trait that encompasses all of these attributes is confidence. It is the quality within us all that, when used to its fullest potential, provides the driving force to reach our ultimate dreams.

In its purest form, confidence is about eliminating the fear of failure and standing up for your beliefs. At times, it becomes difficult when you feel like you can do nothing but succumb to the pressures around you. Confidence, however, provides you with the strength to refute fear, rise up, and make your presence known. In all situations, you have a responsibility to uphold your personal values and expectations. When others choose to do things that are wrong, harmful, or disrespectful, you have an obligation to do the right thing and take action. Failing to live up to those responsibilities and obligations often stems directly from a lack of confidence. In addition, these instances when we fail to uphold our morals cause a depletion of the confidence that does exist. Therefore, it is up to each of us as individuals to develop or enhance the confidence within so we can collectively lead by example in doing what's right.

Confidence is displayed in a variety of different forms. Some people show more of an outward or external confidence that comes through in the way they walk, dress, or talk. Others possess confidence more internally via their intellects or inner strength, which may not show as much from the outside. Some individuals may simply lack confidence or the ability to know how to use it. I appreciate the fact that some people are more timid and apprehensive in life either by nature or because of past experiences. However, the trait of confidence can be harnessed and enhanced with dedication, commitment, and time.

The first step in establishing or developing your confidence is embracing the fact that you deserve nothing but the best that life has to offer. You deserve to be happy, have a great life, and experience everything you hope and dream for. This integral part of confidence is what I like to refer to as "deservability." This idea of "deservability" is at the core of our inner confidence. Everything builds upon this as a foundation for growth and development. Without this inner belief and understanding that you truly are a deserving individual, confidence ceases to exist. An important point to note is that your actions must reflect this ideal of being a deserving person. If you do what's right and make a point to be a good person, that's all it takes. On the other hand, if you take a more selfish approach or do negative things, you don't deserve positivity in return. So, as you live for today, do the right things, lead by example, and embrace the confidence and happiness you truly deserve.

The next step in the process of growing your inner confidence is participating in activities that support your emotional exhilaration. Make a point to ask yourself, "When do I feel I am at my absolute best?" This may be when you are participating in physical exercise, volunteering, teaching, or any other activity that makes you feel energized. By filling our lives with things that makes us feel alive, we are emphasizing the positive while simultaneously eliminating negativity and disappointment. Negativity discourages the development of personal confidence. Therefore, make a point to fill your life with all things positive so that you can realize the strength and excitement that confidence brings.

The final step in the development of confidence is living it every day. Make a point to show the world your eagerness and enthusiasm toward life. If you are excited about having the opportunity to live your life, everyone around you will notice that intensity through your daily interactions. A smile goes a long way toward changing your mood and setting a more positive tone. Refuse to allow any negativity around you to affect you in any way. Be confident about showing your raw emotions, as this invigorates your heart and lets your passion for life shine through.

The most important aspect of growing your confidence is that it must originate and develop from within. We cannot allow ourselves to be dependent on other people or things for our confidence. As you look deep inside yourself, you will begin to understand that you have a purpose and a presence in this world. This emotional connection will cause you to become excited to live life to the fullest. This energy is that driving force I talked about earlier—it is the foundation of strength in your heart and soul. Instead of merely feeling alive while participating in certain activities, develop and enhance your inner confidence so you will feel alive every minute of your life.

As I mentioned previously, we are constantly exposed to the complexities and obstacles of our world. These situations can make the process of growth and development more difficult. In many cases, these challenges become the focal points of our excuses for failing to fulfill our intentions or commitments. After all, when times are tough, it takes relatively no effort to point fingers. However, a strong inner confidence fuels our ability to confront and overcome these hurdles. We need to refuse to make excuses, as they serve no purpose and only hinder progress and improvement.

Some of our biggest challenges in life involve taking chances when the outcome is undefined and uncertain. These situations provide us with opportunities to change our lives for the better and realize new experiences. As you live your life, don't be afraid to take that first risky leap of faith. The joy, pride, and energy you experience from taking that risk is how confidence is born and also how it grows. Too often seeing a task or goal in its entirety seems daunting and overwhelming. This is where many people simply quit and give up. However, by breaking your goals down into smaller components, you will create opportunities for successful outcomes. Create short-term goals, and you will realize short-term victories through your accomplishments. These will generate more positive energy to propel you forward so that in the end, your entire objective will be achieved.

Throughout our daily activities, we also find ourselves involved in making decisions. Some are small and require little thought, while others carry great responsibility and importance. This is another area in our lives where confidence takes on a key role. As you live your life, make a point to act on your gut instinct when tasked with making decisions. This does not mean ignoring facts and pertinent information, but do your best to refrain from overanalyzing, which merely introduces unnecessary complexity and confusion. Your heart is where your gut instinct is born, and your mind is where overanalyzing originates. The minute we begin acting on the thoughts of our minds instead of the feelings of our hearts, we open ourselves to a greater potential for failure and disappointment. Our emotions serve as our guides in telling us what's right, so make a point to listen to the messages they deliver.

We have total control over how we approach all the different forms of complexity in our lives. We can be overwhelmed by them or see them as opportunities and challenges to become better. This comes down to a negative view versus a more positive, optimistic view of the world. In general, negativity seems like a much easier approach than positivity. It is easy to complain, make excuses, and exert little effort in life. This is why people tend to focus more on the negative aspects of their lives and do not make a point to be happy. However, with an inner confidence that you are doing the right thing or making an attempt to do so, you will not be afraid of being different from those who fall into the negativity trap. Some people simply have difficulty recognizing and then doing the right thing. They rely solely on their thoughts or on others' doubts and opinions. In order to understand what's right, you have to listen to your heart and rely on the strong values you stand for. They will always be there to help you make the right decisions and take the best actions.

Once you possess this positive mindset, happiness will simply become a way of life rather than something you have to work for or think about. I've emphasized that confidence is truly about eliminating the fear of failure. In many situations, we may not know exactly what it takes to get something done, but having the confidence to make an attempt is often the biggest hurdle.

Instead of wondering or fearing whether you are doing the right thing, be confident and embrace your drive toward becoming better. As you progress through life, make a point to eliminate excuses and complaints. Instead, see the world and everything in it for what it is and recognize its potential for improvement. Refuse to accept the mentality and approach that life has to be difficult. Life is meant to be natural, easy, and effortless. As you begin to live your life this way, the confidence will start to pour from within. You will carry an energy about you that is contagious to those in your presence. This is the power of the positive.

Life is full of highs and lows, successes and struggles. Our personal lives are filled with situations and circumstances that help guide us down our paths of destiny. Confidence provides us with the spark of determination and enthusiasm to embrace today's opportunities. It gives us the energy to be active leaders in showing the world life's possibilities. With confidence, we develop another key trait that allows us to maintain a focused, positive outlook that can withstand the test of time. I will now discuss the trait of inner strength and its purpose in your journey toward ultimate happiness.

Inner Strength

We all have days we wish never happened and days we wish would never end. The major difference between the overall impacts of these days is how we address and react to these situations. Inner strength allows us to cherish and enjoy every minute of the good times, while learning to persevere and become stronger through the tough times. We often learn most about ourselves in times of hardship, when our feelings and emotions are put to the ultimate test. However, we can also make a point to learn through emotional highs and times of success. After all, should it really take something negative to force us to learn about ourselves or the world around us? When we have an inner strength that empowers us to adapt to life's ups and downs, life becomes much easier and more rewarding.

So this idea of inner strength—what exactly does it mean, and how does it fit in the puzzle of life? In its simplest form, inner strength is that special emotion in our hearts that pushes us in all aspects of our lives. It provides us with the stability and support to never give up. Inner strength is fueled by the confidence we acquire from working hard, overcoming obstacles, and being successful. As we make a point to be good people and do positive things, our inner strength grows even stronger. We rely on it as our guiding inspiration to reach higher, even after our greatest accomplishments.

Inner strength also provides us with a stable foundation of protection and comfort when we need it most. Sometimes when life gets us down, we have a desire to give up and quit. This is simply due to the fact that it is easier to do so. It is much more difficult to push through and be strong when confronted with life's challenges. Overcoming these hurdles requires the strength, confidence, and perseverance that are within us all. Your heart and soul have the capacity for encompassing all of these traits, but it is up to you to develop them to their fullest potential. As you do so, you will find them to be your most trusted assets in your daily pursuits.

As we live our lives, we surround ourselves with people we love and trust to share our successes and support us through our struggles. These individuals provide us with external assistance and guidance to make things easier. However, inner strength is strictly about you and eliminates the need for other people or circumstances to push you through. There are times in all our lives when our families and friends are not present to help us. These difficult times require tapping that inner strength and handling the situations on our own. If we harness the strength and confidence that lies within, any additional support we receive from others becomes an added benefit rather than a necessity. Without emotionally strong spirits, we lack the ability to help others when they are in need. However, as you develop your inner strength, you can begin to share it with others so that they too can become stronger.

Now that we have a deeper understanding of inner strength, it's important to discuss how to enhance it. The process of growing your inner strength is no different from any of the other traits I have previously discussed. It takes a commitment to opening yourself up and making the most of every opportunity to improve.

The first step in the development of your inner strength is being confident in yourself and trusting your instincts to guide you. You have the tools you need to make the right decisions, so use them for all things positive. As you begin to act on these principles, you will realize happiness through doing what's right. Too often our minds become consumed with thoughts of doubt when we fail to live up to our personal expectations. Instead of carrying around the burden of doubt, enjoy the freedom and relief that doing the right thing brings. After all, when you make a point to do what you feel is right, you no longer have to wonder about what you didn't do or what you could have done. The stress and frustration we put on ourselves merely brings us down and inhibits the attraction of positive thoughts. However, the process of freeing our minds both strengthens our souls and inspires us to have ideas for even greater possibilities.

These inspired thoughts are the foundation for the next step in growing your inner strength. More specifically, the second piece of the process is making a point to improve on a personal level. No one in this world is perfect in any way, and we all have traits and qualities that can be enhanced. As we improve as individuals, we concurrently develop more confidence, strength, and happiness through each and every experience. The process of personal development allows us to understand ourselves on a much deeper level. The more we know about ourselves, the better suited we are to live our lives and contribute to the world around us.

The world of positivity is about focusing on becoming a better individual in all facets of life. In order to become better, we must approach each and every situation with a positive mindset. We all have times in our lives when something negative happens that directly affects us on a personal level. For example, if someone close to you passes away, you must take something from that experience and become better because of it. Fill your thoughts with the positive attributes and qualities that person brought to your life and be sure to always keep them with you. On the other hand, it is equally important to show appreciation and gratitude for all the positive things that happen in our lives. Make a point to be thankful for each opportunity and use every experience to drive you toward even more. If we, as individuals in our societies, are not focused on becoming stronger and driven to improve ourselves for the future, life's experiences pass us by without adding true value. Everything happens for a reason, whether we choose to accept it or not. However, by taking the positive from every situation, we grow and develop every day we're given the gift of living our lives.

During one of my engineering courses in college, I learned about kaizen, a manufacturing philosophy that I found very interesting. Kaizen is a Japanese word that means continuous and incremental improvement. The principle behind this philosophy is to conduct activities that promote improvement in all aspects of the process, business, or entity at hand. Today, several businesses all over the world use principles related to or directly pulled from the origins of kaizen. As I learned more about this philosophy, I was intrigued by the simple and fundamental concepts that kaizen represents and how closely they relate to life in general. As we look to the future, we all must focus on continuous improvement so that we become stronger and better prepared for everything still to come. In doing so, our personal development will collectively promote the world's advancement and growth.

It's an interesting and unique idea to continually improve in all aspects of your life through everything you do. Briefly pause and think about this concept for a second. If you make a point of becoming better each day, your last day is guaranteed to be your best day. What better way to leave this world than at your absolute best? This is the power of the positive.

So now that we've made a point to trust ourselves, rely on our instincts, and make a commitment to improve, the question becomes: how do we make these qualities last? As I've discussed, the lives we live are full of both highs and lows—good times and bad. One word that I like to use when discussing the importance and development of inner strength is "sustainability." Sustainability is about withstanding the test of time and persevering in all situations. It also means accentuating the highs while conquering and overpowering the lows. When things aren't going your way, your thoughts become consumed by doubt and failure. You want nothing more than to put an end to those feelings of hopelessness and despair. Tapping your inner strength provides that boost of energy you need to push through and continue moving forward. Each time you overcome an obstacle, you further enhance your inner strength for the next time it's needed. It is through this process of continually overcoming life's hurdles that your personal sustainability develops.

Living up to your personal priorities and expectations also helps to enhance your inner strength. The execution of such consistency in being your best and doing what's right strengthens your core foundation. This consistency also helps expand your inner strength to serve as your greatest asset and support when you need it most. After all, having inner strength one day that is no longer present the next serves no purpose. However, having sustained inner strength allows you to maintain positive energy and a positive attitude every day you live your life.

Businesses all around the world deal with sustainability on a daily basis. They are working to stay competitive in the ever-changing marketplace, and sustainability provides them with that stable foundation

I spoke of earlier. Both in times of success and hardship, businesses rely on their solid frameworks to hold them together and allow them to persevere. Billions of dollars are spent each year on new technologies that help strengthen business infrastructures. Those companies that lack strong foundations and support systems are those that cease to exist when times get tough. It's easy to be strong for the short-term future or in times of prosperity, but sustainability is about preserving your existence for the duration.

Continuous and sustainable improvement develops and enhances the inner strength within us all. I'd like to summarize this trait of inner strength with an example. I was only nine years old at the time, but I still remember March of 1993, when former North Carolina State men's basketball coach, Jim Valvano, received the Arthur Ashe Courage Award at the ESPY Awards. Jim was faced with a cancer that would take his life less than two months later, but he wanted people to know how important it was to always give everything you had and to never quit. His cancer research foundation's motto uses a portion of his message that night: "Don't give up; don't ever give up." Jim emphasized how important it is to enjoy your life, work hard to make your dreams come true, and be appreciative of every moment you have. He also described three things that we should all do each and every day. Jim said you have to laugh, engage your mind in thought, and "have your emotions moved to tears." Instead of talking strictly about courage and accepting his award, Jim made the most of the opportunity by sharing a positive message with the world. His words had a great effect on those watching that night and still do today.

At that time, being so young, I simply took the speech for what it was and watched the rest of the show. However, through this process of self-improvement, I've reflected back on that experience and have afforded it a much deeper meaning. During this process, I made a point to ask myself what I thought about each of the three components Jim spoke about. I summarized the impressions his speech made on me and decided which lessons from that experience I would share with you. First, laugh each day—be happy in life, and show others your happiness. You will find that people are strongly attracted to you because of it, and they too will start to show their happiness. Second, spend time in thought— make a point to develop your awareness and appreciation for the world around you. Finally, make a point to show emotion—if you need to smile, smile; if you need to cry, cry. Show others you care about them and never be afraid to tell them so. Do not take those you cherish in your life for granted, because they can be gone in an instant, leaving no further opportunities to tell them how much they mean to you. After all, it is through this process of emitting our raw emotions that our true characters and passions shine through.

That night, Jim was a living symbol of everything inner strength represents. He wasn't afraid of the cancer or the thought of dying from it. He focused solely on living in the moment and fighting for the gift of life he'd been given. This is but one example of the many stories of inspiration, strength, and hope in our world.

As you continue on your journey of self-improvement, take time to think about what constitutes a great day in your eyes. Have confidence, engage yourself, and be passionate in everything you do in life. No matter what happens, you can never give up or compromise who you are and where you want to go. When life knocks you down, make a point to stand up and try again. Use your inner strength to overcome your life's obstacles. This perseverance will push you to enjoy the successes and rewards of your greatest accomplishments.

Among all the traits I discuss throughout this book, one common theme exists: take life's experiences to the individual level and search within to find your presence and purpose. We've all been given the proper tools and skills to live a great life, but we sometimes struggle to put it all together and make it happen. My goal is to provide you with a new outlook to reveal your path of destiny. From there, it is entirely up to you to take this path to your ultimate happiness and success. Since the core of personal development is the individual, I would like to further discuss the importance of upholding and enhancing your true self. In a world filled with such complexity, preserving your independence is an integral component of your progression through life. With that, I will now explain the next trait, independence.

INDEPENDENCE

Although this world is comprised of different nations, societies, communities, and families, there is something much simpler at hand. In its simplest form, this world is comprised of individuals. We are all unique; in other words, not one of us is the same as any other. From a positive perspective, this is truly a great thing that we must learn to appreciate. A world filled with such variety and diversity can make it difficult to see others for who they are instead of who they are not. Too often our differences become our justification for disagreement and separation instead of our drive for collaboration and unity. As I've said before, we all have strengths, and we all have weaknesses. We don't choose this; it is simply how we were put together. Naturally, we learn to rely on one another, but it is so important to be independent at the same time.

Independence means so many things in so many different contexts, so I want to clarify what it means to me in the way that I live my life. To put it simply, I believe independence is about being a self-sufficient individual first and being everything else second. This by no means entails being a selfish person, but merely emphasizes the importance of helping yourself so you are fully prepared and capable to help others.

Throughout our daily lives, we all take on a wide variety of roles and titles. At any given time, each of us may be a son or daughter, a brother or sister, a mother or father, an employee or boss, and so on. Each of these roles brings with it a set of responsibilities and obligations. However, in order to be good at each of these roles, we must be good as individuals first and foremost. We have no hope to have a positive effect on others without a solid internal foundation. Your independence also helps support your inner strength, drive, and personal expectations. When these fundamentals are sound, you will create opportunities to contribute positively to those around you. Without a stable foundation, your message becomes unclear, and your potential for positive change is weakened.

One of the keys to independence is removing the unnecessary conditions and constraints we put on others and ourselves. Prime examples of these constraints are those we place on our personal happiness. For example, if I can be happy in life, experiencing and enjoying all that life has to offer, my happiness lies within me. If I also have a great group of friends and family who make my life even better, their effect on me is an added benefit; not a necessity. Most of us want our family members and friends to bring this added joy and support, but we cannot allow our personal happiness to be solely dependent on others. This is where preserving your independence becomes so important. Too often people place their happiness in the hands of another individual or group of individuals, which only leads to opportunities for disappointment. In other cases, people set constraints or expectations that they feel they have to meet in order to truly be happy. Conditional happiness often causes people to be continually frustrated because they establish opportunities for unsuccessful outcomes. However, when your happiness lies within, your dependence on others and the world around you is greatly reduced. By removing these unnecessary constraints and expectations, you establish the potential for more positive results. Ultimately, if we can all be happy on our own, our experiences will only be enriched by the support we receive from others in our lives.

Just like happiness, your inner strength and confidence must be free of conditional constraints. As you focus your efforts and energy on enhancing your independence, you free yourself of comparisons to others around you. I mentioned previously that we are all unique, so comparing yourself to others truly serves no purpose. Let your personal expectations that you have set for yourself be your guide and your benchmark for your success in life. Feel the freedom from removing the pressures of society from your life, and refuse to allow them to alter the values you stand for. As I discussed earlier, we naturally become complaisant and find ourselves relying on others to fulfill certain needs in our lives. This is only a positive situation if we maintain our independence. If something were to adversely affect the connection we have with someone, the obstacle can and will be overcome. We must always retain the confidence that we will make it through any situation that arises during the course of our lives. Throughout life, as you meet and exceed your personal expectations, the inner strength and confidence within you grows. This is the power of the positive.

Independence is also about freeing yourself from using other people or situations as cover-ups or distractions from addressing the real problems in your life. Too often we make excuses as to why things are the way they are when, in reality, the deeper truth tells a different story.

I see these situations falling into one of two problem categories that I like to refer to as "patches" and "crutches." Let me further explain each of these and how they relate to your personal independence.

First of all, "patches." Patches are when we disguise the truth to avoid confronting the real problem. For example, if you accidentally put a hole in the wall, moving a plant in front of it only serves as a cover-up. The problem is never resolved until the hole in the wall is repaired. Every day you walk by it, you subconsciously are disappointed in yourself. This same situation applies to relationships with other people. We often suppress our true emotions when times are tough instead of being open and honest about how we feel. We tell the other person or group of people involved that everything is okay when, in reality, it is not. Withholding these feelings leads to a more violent eruption of emotions at a later time. In many cases, this large outburst occurs over something small, and it all stems back to that initial instance of emotional suppression. In these situations, we often put the blame on the person or situation causing the current frustration. However, we should be putting the blame on ourselves for not being open and sharing our feelings from the beginning. As you proceed through your personal growth and development, make a point to step back in all situations, good and bad. Take the time to understand the true root cause of the problem, and be humble enough to personally accept the blame if it is justified. Rely on your instincts, and trust your heart to tell you what is right. Maintain your independence, and do not allow the presence or pressures of others to distract you from addressing the truth. Instead of putting the plant in front of the dent in the wall, take the time to fix it. You will feel better about yourself and gain confidence from simply doing the right thing. Instead of suppressing your true feelings, be open and honest with others about how they make you feel. This gives them an opportunity to make things better, and those who matter will embrace the opportunity.

Now, the second category that many personal issues often fall into is "crutches." Crutches are the people or things we use to help us get through life's troubles without addressing the real issue at hand. As an example, imagine yourself as a student in a group project or an employee on a team assignment for your company. You may have a problem because of individuals who are failing to perform and carry their weight. In this situation, you have two options: confront the individuals about the problem, or serve as a crutch and pick up the extra work yourself. Many people often like to avoid any type of confrontation and take the easy route by serving as a crutch. The right thing to do in this case is to maintain your independence and be confident. Be open and honest about the situation at hand. In many instances, this involves telling people something they do not necessarily want to hear. However, just as before, those who matter and truly care will step up, pull their weight, and make a point to improve. Part of your personal independence involves the elimination of crutches you may be using in your life as well as the avoidance of situations in which you are serving as a crutch. Using other people or things as a crutch prevents you from relieving certain burdens from your subconscious. On the other hand, by serving as a crutch, you never give other people the opportunity to improve or understand that what they are doing is wrong. In either case, you hinder the growth and development of yourself and/or others.

Each and every day we are confronted with making decisions that represent who we are and the values we stand for. The choices we make directly reflect our personal approaches to life and the types of impact we want to make. In the business world, many decisions often come back to answering one key question: does the topic at hand add value to the customer? Businesses want and need to ensure that what they are pursuing is truly value-added to the consumer. If a new technology or means of doing business brings no additional benefit or improvement, businesses usually decide to forgo that option. This same concept applies to life in general and those decisions we make as individuals on a daily basis. We must make a point to base our decisions on choosing the option that brings the most value to each situation. When tasked with confronting complications or misfortunes, we often seek the easiest solution. In most cases, this easy solution is neither the right solution nor the one that adds true value. Too often, people allow their minds to run wild with meaningless and untruthful justifications for problems in their lives. This is where the patches and crutches that I discussed earlier come in. At the core of both patches and crutches are excuses and complaints, neither of which serves any purpose. When you make an excuse or complain about the way something is or is not, do you ever ask yourself what good it does to you or anyone else? Making a negative statement or contriving artificial reasoning for something adds no value in life and, in fact, hinders growth and progress. As you live your life, instead of making complaints and excuses, ask yourself what you can do to positively impact each particular issue or situation. In doing so, you will reallocate the time and energy that was being wasted to instead fuel your drive and commitment for making things better. Ensure that everything you do is valuable, and refuse to be involved in anything that contradicts this philosophy. Always remember, a life without excuses is a life full of promise.

To further explain the importance of independence, I would like to share another connection to the world of positivity and one of its influential figures. Positive thinking has been in existence for centuries, conceivably as long as there has been human thought. The efforts and teachings of others have made great strides in the evolution of humankind. Ralph Waldo Emerson, a famous philosopher of the nineteenth century, taught others in his time about the concept and effects of positive thinking. Emerson was a firm believer in living a simple life in harmony with others while preserving individual independence. A favorite Emerson quote of mine is, "It is one of the most beautiful compensations in life … that no man can sincerely try to help another without helping himself." I feel that this quote summarizes my thoughts in a single sentence and explains that we cannot forget to think about ourselves if we hope to have a positive effect on others. If a math teacher is not good at math, how valuable is she as a teacher to her students? The same holds true for life in general. If we are not the best we can be as individuals, how can we positively affect others in society and the world we live in? As a parent, if you are not the type of person you want your children to be, can you truly expect them to uphold the morals and values that you fail to live up to? By embracing who we are as individuals and continually improving ourselves, we establish both the potential and the ability to help others. We learn more about who we are, which helps us have a greater understanding of our roles in the world around us. Leading by example and living your daily life as a good person speak more than you could ever say through words.

Independence plays an integral role in realizing the power of the positive and living it every day. No one knows what the future may bring and whether or not the people and things we cherish each day will be present tomorrow. As you continue your journey through life, preserve and enhance your independence so that you too can make a positive impression. Eliminate the excuses, patches, and crutches from all aspects of your life. Never allow yourself to take the free ride or the easy ride in life. Embrace the challenges of today and use them to strengthen your soul. The struggles you encounter and overcome are what develop you as an independent individual. They help serve as your guide down your path of destiny.

Before we proceed to the next section of the book, I'd like you to answer the following questions:

What does independence mean to you as an individual? Are there areas in your life where you feel more independent than others? Do you find yourself relying on other people or things for you to feel good about yourself? Are you being fully open and honest with yourself and others? Do you use patches or crutches in your life to avoid addressing problems? Are there situations in which you are serving as a patch or crutch, preventing others from growth and development?

Take the time to think about these questions and your responses to them. In doing so, you'll continue to learn more about yourself, areas your independence shines through, and areas where it needs attention for further improvement.

This idea of independence and what it represents is very simple. Hold strong to who you are and grow as an individual. Doing your best to remove the world's unnecessary pressures, expectations, and complications is all part of the development process. Your heart will lead you in creating a path for personal success and embracing your potential for doing what's right. The intimate nature of independence leads me to explain the next trait in living a positive life, simplicity.

SIMPLICITY

The human mind is truly amazing in every sense of its power and potential. It is constantly at work, engaging with anything and everything our subconscious permits. It is very easy for our minds to be consumed in so many different things that they naturally become overloaded. However, life can be very simple. We must decide for ourselves how simple or complex we want our lives to be. Too often I see people who are so caught up in the unnecessary complexities of their lives that they become overwhelmed. Simplicity is a solution to many of life's problems, and using it for all things positive makes all the difference in the world.

The integration of this trait into your daily life is a process, just like all the others. However, with a strong sense of dedication and self-discipline, you too can realize the freedom and peace of living a simple life. The journey at times may be difficult, but the end result is worth your time and effort. The first step in the process of simplifying your life is sorting things out to determine what's most important.

The essence of the positive mindset is about keeping things simple and focusing our efforts on the things that truly matter. Life itself dictates that we have a finite amount of time during the course of each day. We often wish there were more than twenty-four hours in a day, but, unfortunately, that just isn't something that will be changing anytime soon. With this in mind, we all must focus our time and energy on the things that make us happy and the things we feel are most important. In doing so, we will embrace the feelings of personal fulfillment and pride from making the most of every opportunity. Unfortunately, I see people who focus so much of their energy on the negative aspects of their lives that they simply have nothing left for positivity and happiness. As you live your life, are you focusing your time and energy each day on the positive or the negative? If you find yourself answering with the latter, ask yourself what benefit or pleasure you receive from doing so. By simply reallocating your efforts to the positive things that truly matter, you will find yourself much happier and more fulfilled.

Even though time is a fixed entity in this world, the energy we have can grow and expand as we engage our hearts in our lives' true passions. When you are enthusiastic about what you are doing, you embrace a feeling that you never want to stop. This positive emotion fuels your drive to do even more. In essence, we all have the ability to add to our personal energy supply simply by doing things that make us happy. We also have the opportunity to make our contribution toward a better life for all mankind. If you concentrate your efforts on making the best use of your time and continually adding to the energy that lies within, you've done your part. Then, as everyone else in society does the same, we can collectively realize a world beyond our wildest imaginations. This is the power of the positive.

Now that you've made a commitment to focus your attention on the positive, you have an obligation to live it every day. The second step in the process of simplifying your life is aligning your daily activities with your personal priorities. We have to ensure that everything we are spending time on and exerting energy toward directly reflects those priorities. This is exactly what the "live your priorities" concept that I discussed earlier in the book is all about. If part of who you are is focused on being happy, your pursuits each day should be living examples of that principle. Living your priorities shows others your true colors and tells them your personal story. It is our responsibility to fill our lives with the positive so that we can be happy today and each day to come. After all, happiness isn't something we should be constantly waiting for—it's an experience for this time and this moment. Unfortunately, we are also responsible for removing those aspects of our daily endeavors that fail to meet our personal expectations and priorities. This is often the most critical and difficult part of the process. The struggles with this responsibility often stem from the complexity, or lack of simplicity, we've developed in our lives. The evolution of technological advances has definitely contributed to this complication.

The options we have nowadays for just about everything in life are truly amazing. Therefore, it is a little more challenging to sort them all out and keep things simple. As time goes on, we find ourselves immersed in a world with new innovations and products that are all supposed to make our lives better and easier. However, when you consider the abundance of such items available to us, the number of options can get out of hand rather quickly. Take a close look at the cereal aisle in your local grocery store, and you'll know exactly what I mean. In addition, the pressures of society and those around us often force us to make rash decisions and choices. We buy things because everyone else has one or because it's new and popular. However, is it really anyone else's fault if we become stressed and overwhelmed by the decisions or purchases we make? This is again where simplicity plays an integral role. We all have an obligation to ourselves to determine the extent of these niceties we incorporate into our lives. We constantly make decisions about who and what we want to include in our lives. Ultimately we are responsible for those decisions and the results that follow. Over the course of time, the accumulation of everything we possess can become difficult to manage. This is why it's important at times to take a step back and take inventory of your life. Whether it's the material items you possess or the personal relationships you have with others, there are always opportunities to simplify. This is the third and final step in the process of simplifying your life: removing the unnecessary complexities. As I mentioned earlier, this is often the most critical and difficult part. It's hard to let things go because of the emotional attachments we have with our personal belongings and those around us. However, we have an obligation to ourselves, and we have to stay focused on the big picture. Making the right decisions isn't always easy, but your inner voice will be there to guide you. It will help show you the way and be the support when you need it most. Moving forward, we will look back on these times of simplifying our lives and making the tough decisions with appreciation that we followed our hearts in doing what's right.

In addition to removing the unnecessary complexities, it's important to remove sources of negativity as well. These sources can be just about anything, including people, society's pressures, or the constraints we put on ourselves. Living a positive life is about freeing yourself of such negativity and its burdens. Think of negatives as obstacles in your path of destiny. They are roadblocks that prevent your heart from showing you your life's true passions and purpose. If we remove these distractions and focus that energy instead on listening to our raw emotions and feelings, we will create an opportunity to find such happiness. By keeping things simple, we open our hearts to inspired thoughts, creative ideas, and a better way of living.

So, in this complex world we live in, how do we hold strong to the positive and let go of the negative? It's an important question to ask when trying to simplify your life, so I'll share my response with you. Each and every day that we are given a new opportunity, we are continually acting as filters. In general, anything that is filtered enters as an input and exits as an output. The difference between the two is what gets removed in the process. Everything around us can be considered an input to our personal lives. Our values, priorities, and expectations encompass the filter for each of those inputs. The outputs are the resulting actions and decisions we make each day. As individuals, we decide how we will allow our surroundings to affect our thoughts, our spirits, and our approaches to our lives. This is how our daily life filtration processes work. We decide what gets through to our souls and what stops on the outside. As I mentioned before, we often become overburdened with pressures from others or ourselves. Instead of filtering out these negative inputs, we often allow those pressures to alter our personal expectations. However, we can only blame ourselves for failing to uphold the values we represent. I'd like to illustrate this concept with an example that everyone can relate to. Let's say that during the course of your day someone makes a negative remark about the way you look. This is an input to your personal life. Immediately and instinctively your subconscious makes a decision about your reaction to such a comment. In making that decision, your mind and your heart use those principles you stand for as its filter. As a positive person who is confident and proud of who you are, you decide that the comment fails to represent those values. You leave it on the surface and don't allow it to come inside and affect your inner beliefs. You move on with your life and learn from that experience to help you address potential situations that may arise in the future. In doing so, you gain even more confidence from standing up for who you are and refusing to allow such negativity into your life. Examples like these are endless; unfortunately, we can be confronted with them almost daily. However, it's so important to stay true to who we are and filter out anything that deviates from our core foundation.

As I mentioned earlier, our minds are more powerful than most people ever realize. I can speak from personal experiences when the thoughts and visions I had became reality by simply focusing on them. I continue to fill my mind and my heart with the dreams and goals that drive my passions in life. As I write this book, I am consumed by the thought of you reading it someday and of fulfilling my vision of being a successful author. It is so important to understand this concept that our minds have the ability to work with our hearts to create the futures we desire. Once you make this connection, the possibilities become endless. Incorporating simplicity into your life allows you to free your mind of the unnecessary aspects of our world. In doing so, you will embrace a sense of openness and understanding of your thoughts and emotions.

This sense of ease that simplicity brings also introduces another key aspect of its application—flexibility. This trait represents the freedom to make positive advances in your life. It becomes so important to be flexible and welcome the change that life brings. We all possess the ability to adapt and improve simply by taking a positive approach. Without such flexibility, our lives become rigid, stagnant, and dull. With it, however, we create new opportunities and promote excitement, variety, and interest.

It is also important to understand that simplicity surrounds us in everything we do. It can be applied in all aspects of our lives and has even become very popular in the world of business. Companies of all sizes work at great lengths to simplify the way they do business. Simplification of processes, communication, travel, and the like all help makes things easier. Complexities in business foster and disguise problems, both of which hinder progress and development. I've used the analogy before that your life is like your own personal business with you as the owner. Through living this approach, you will begin to remove the obstacles and clutter that prevent you from reaching your true potential. After all, do you want your life to be easy, simple, and focused or difficult, complex, and distracted? The choice is yours. The concept of simplicity is fundamental, but the execution is our challenge.

As you continue on your course of self-improvement, think of simplicity as the tool to clean up your life. Use it for all things positive to establish a system in which your life feels natural and organized. It can be very easy to allow ourselves to become consumed by the abundance of life. However, if we use simplicity in our approach to focus the energy that we have on the priorities that matter most, life becomes much easier and more rewarding. The key is to not be afraid to live a simple life that involves fewer "things" to occupy your mind; instead, concentrate on the few essentials that you would never want to live without. Simplicity may be different from the norm of society, but being different is never a bad thing. As you pursue the opportunities and challenges in life, make a point to keep things simple. As I previously mentioned, the goals you set may be difficult and ambitious, but breaking them down into more feasible milestones will help immensely. These will provide you with short-term successes and propel you toward reaching your ultimate dreams.

Up to this point, I have discussed several traits that collectively incorporate the philosophies of living a positive life. Each of them contributes something different to the overall process. However, without one key trait, the potential for developing all the others ceases to exist. Embracing the power of the positive is contingent on the approach you choose to take each day you live your life. With a view of the world that is filled with hope, potential, and prosperity, your path of destiny will become clear. The trait that embodies these principles is optimism, the trait I will now discuss.

Optimism

It all starts with a belief, an inner-knowing, and a feeling of something special. This conviction, that anything truly is possible, establishes the foundation for living a life of dreams. With it, the world becomes an open door toward endless opportunities. Without it, the experience of life merely serves as a passage of time. As you look to your future, do you firmly believe that you have a purpose? How will you choose to make your mark and have your presence remembered for generations to come? While considering your response to these questions, keep one thing in mind. The opportunities are here today and the decisions are yours to make.

Living a positive life is about making good choices and doing the right things. To some this concept seems elementary, easy, and effortless. However, one of the most important decisions we all face in life is one that many people often struggle with. This decision does not involve college, marriage, or even a career. The decision I am referring to is much simpler than that—it is how we approach this world we live in. We have two options: we can either approach life with the mindset that we are going to make the most of this amazing opportunity and live life to the fullest, or we can wake up each day and let our surroundings decide how our life will play out. The first is centered on confidence, hope, and positivity—the second on fear, doubt, and negativity. This decision is critical for shaping your path in life, so trust your heart and let optimism be your guide.

As I began this amazing journey to change my life for the better, this is exactly where I began. I subconsciously knew that before I did anything else, I first had to change my outlook on life. Up to that point, I was more of a pessimist and struggled to accept things for what they were. I viewed the world for what it was lacking instead of seeing its potential. For example, I saw people for their faults and imperfections rather than their contributions and talents. Difficult situations were seen as problems instead of opportunities. This approach all changed, however, when I decided to improve my life. Rather than imposing judgment and being critical of my surroundings, I instead chose to embrace an appreciation for everything around me. In doing so, I began to develop an open awareness of the prosperity and promise in life.

When tasked with deciding how I would approach this opportunity, the answer became clear. The choice I made was to set a positive tone for each day and make the most of every moment I had. I made a point to ensure positivity was the basis behind my thoughts, feelings, and actions. Now, as I wake up each morning, I am grateful for another day and focus my efforts on making it special. This is what fuels the drive and passion within me to make my positive mark on whatever comes my way. I later reflect and evaluate whether I made the most of the day, or the day made the most of me. Since that first moment when I consciously made a point to take a positive approach to life, I have considered each day a true success. This is the power of the positive.

Unfortunately, I see too many people who wake up each morning wondering what may happen to them during the course of their day, often fearing the worst. These individuals take the alternative approach to life and allow the tone for their day to be set by their surroundings. They place the power in others' hands to determine the ultimate success or failure of their day. If you are one of these people, today is your opportunity to change this. After all, who do you want to be in control of your personal happiness—yourself or the world around you? Instead of waking up with a fear of what's to come, instead embrace the confidence that you can make each day great. I guarantee that by consciously making a point to view your day optimistically, you will see drastic changes in your overall happiness.

So, that's where it starts. Set a positive tone for the day to get you headed down the right track. It then becomes imperative to live that positive message throughout your daily activities. As I've mentioned previously, your thoughts and words tell one story, but your actions show your true colors. They help paint the picture of your life and serve as your contribution to the world. I also firmly believe that what you put out, you will receive back. Therefore, those who emit positive energy receive positive energy in return. To put it simply, if you do good things in life, more will naturally come your way as a result. I have personally felt the effects of living this ideal each day. People see firsthand that I am a positive person, and those around me respond well to the happiness and enthusiasm I display. This is a form of direct feedback that my message to the outside world is well received. Take a moment and think about the message you deliver each day and the impression you leave on those around you. Are people grateful and inspired or resentful and frustrated by your presence in life? Your answer to this question will clearly show you the theme of your life story. Each new day carries the potential for greatness, so show your appreciation by making a positive impact.

This notion of optimism seems simple and appealing to some, yet others still take a negative and pessimistic approach to life. So, given the opportunity to decide for yourself, why would you choose negativity over positivity? In order to fully answer this question, it is important to first understand the difference between the positive and the negative. Negativity, in its truest form, is simply looking at things from a perspective of absence or void. By that, I mean everything is focused on what's wrong, what something is not, or what doesn't exist. This is where words like should, could, and would originate— directly from the negative. They imply both a sense of judgment and opinion. In a similar manner, complaints and excuses also stem from the negative mindset. They serve no purpose in solving the problems of our world and instead inhibit the formation of their solutions. It's understandable that when life gets tough, we sometimes need to vent and get things out. However, the key is to not simply complain, but instead to voice your frustration along with your plan of action to positively affect that situation. Sources of negativity infiltrate our minds, our hearts, and our souls when we fail to take a positive approach to life. Times of boredom and mind searching create opportunities for the negative to interject. Optimism, on the other hand, establishes an environment where we can think creatively, strengthen our successes, and overcome our shortcomings. With a view of what's right in the world, we can positively affect and change the things we desire to improve. The optimistic mindset immerses our thoughts and emotions in positivity, which simultaneously extinguishes the potential for negativity.

Now that we have a deeper understanding of the differences between the positive and the negative, let's get back to the question at hand. Why would someone choose negativity over positivity? First, it is important to keep in mind that we are all different from one another. We all have values, backgrounds, and life stories that are unique to each of us. Therefore, we can never truly relate or understand exactly where someone else is coming from. Some people may simply be negative because it's all they've ever known. They may have had troubled childhoods or been surrounded by negative people growing up. Therefore, we have no right to make judgments about other people's views of the world or their approaches to life. However, we can live our lives in a positive manner and allow them to see a different perspective. Those who wish to change and improve will embrace this new outlook on life. Positivity, however, is not the way everyone chooses to live life, so some will refuse to change. The only control we have is how we live our lives. We can't make decisions for others, but we can be living examples of life's true goodness.

Despite all our differences as human beings, we collectively share commonalities that unite us. We see these similarities when we take a look at our overall society and the qualities it represents. Unfortunately, we live in a world that focuses more on the negative and less on the positive. As an example, think about the themes or major headlines when you turn on the nightly news. It seems as if all you hear about are the crimes, misfortunes, and downfalls of the day. Throughout the course of time we have unfortunately developed a strange curiosity about the negative. Our minds have become consumed with acquiring information that usually has no impact on our daily lives. In reality, such information merely serves as a distraction from our personal focus on life. This is what has to change, and now is the time to change it. Let's use our unique curiosity to dream big, solve problems, and find the positive in all situations. After all, how different would it be to turn on that same news channel and hear the uplifting success stories and acts of kindness displayed by those who do what's right in this world? Regardless of our personal histories, we all possess the opportunity to make positive change for the future.

So how do we make such a change and shift the focus of our society to the positive? To change the world in a positive way requires ingraining happiness and goodwill in everything that we do. Individually, we can change our personal lives, but as a whole, we can make this a better place for the future. There are signs that we're starting to pave the way in a better direction. Lyrics to current music, concepts for new television shows, and other representations of society's values are encouraging more people to live great lives and help others to do the same. Songs such as "If Today Was Your Last Day", by Nickleback, and "Someday", by Rob Thomas, promote making the most of today's opportunities. In addition, Oprah Winfrey has created an entire network dedicated to new shows that spread the message of positivity and inspire people to live their best lives. The key is that we each need to do our part in serving our world. As we collectively work together toward a common goal, we make positive strides toward the betterment of this amazing place.

So how do we measure progress in such endeavors? As individuals, we can self-reflect and evaluate the state of our personal happiness. However, how do we as a global universe assess these same qualities? I found myself attempting to formalize a response to this question and one day found a possible solution. I watched a television special with Michael J. Fox called *Adventures of an Incurable Optimist.* Fox was diagnosed with Parkinson's disease in 1991 at the age of thirty. He has since tried to make the most of every opportunity to find a cure for this disease. This particular special was about Fox's quest to discover why some individuals are optimistic and to understand the effects of living life with such an approach. Part of the documentary chronicled Fox's trip to a small nation in South Asia called Bhutan, which is a country where happiness is a focal point and a priority. The people of Bhutan take great pride in their well-being and quality of life. Nations all around the world, including Bhutan, measure economic performance through indicators like gross-national product (GNP). These indicators focus on trade and business-related activities rather than on the psychological state of a nation's population. Bhutan thought so highly of the personal satisfaction and wellness of its people that its leaders developed a new economic index called gross-national happiness, or GNH. This allows them to track and analyze how their people feel about themselves and the environment in which they live. Later in the special, Fox noted that being immersed in such a positive environment reduced the affect of his symptoms and made him feel better. This is just one example of developing new ways of focusing our attention on what truly matters. It also shows how each of us can do something special and share positive messages of happiness and goodwill. If Fox, and others all around the world with serious illnesses, can stay strong and optimistic about the future, the rest of us can surely do the same.

As we continue to move forward in life, it becomes clear that our world has a passion and a desire for progress. This trait of optimism serves as a key principle in the philosophy of kaizen, or continuous improvement, which I discussed earlier. Without an optimistic view of the world, your desire to improve ceases to exist and life stagnates in monotony. However, with it, your ambition and dedication shine through. As you commit yourself to constant growth and development, you simultaneously become better as an individual. I know that in general, most people wish to improve and be happy. Their success depends on how important improvement and happiness are to them and the strength of their commitment.

Throughout this discussion, you may be wondering where the positivity and optimism in your life stem from and how you can realize their fullest potentials. The answer lies in the same place as all the other traits I've discussed throughout the book. Positivity is a form of love, and this love emanates from your heart. In a sense, positivity is the generator of the strong and joyous emotions we feel when we do what's right. Optimism is our gateway or the tool we use in order to reach such happiness. To put it even simpler, positivity, and everything it represents, establishes the possibility of living a life of dreams. Taking an optimistic approach each day serves as your means to attain your dreams. When times get tough, you can always return to your heart and find the love that's always there. Trust it, and use all its power to get you right back on track toward the life you know so well. No matter what happens, always remember that love lives inside your heart and not within your mind. As time passes, the achievements of your mind will fade to moments of your past, but the accomplishments of your heart will emerge as memories of your lifetime.

As you embrace today's opportunities, make a point to take the right approach. Failure to take a specific approach in life creates the potential for any outcome that may come your way. However, by choosing optimism, you guarantee a successful outcome. The positive isn't always easy to uncover, especially in times of great hardship, but remember that it's always there. You just need to find it.

Each day we encounter new situations, and how we react to those situations is very important. Since we are all different individuals, we see things differently and thus respond differently. As you continue your journey in life, learn to accept those around you for who they are. Appreciate their good qualities, and do your best to understand their points of view. In doing so, you'll also learn more about yourself and your personal outlook on life.

Create an environment that welcomes peace and happiness into your life. Engage yourself in positive situations and do your best to eliminate sources of negativity. Share your optimistic view of the world with others who struggle to see the possibility and potential life offers. Do your best to see life's experiences as opportunities to learn and grow. These will prepare you for everything that comes your way in the future. Preparation eliminates the need for worry, doubt, and uncertainty. Instead, such preparation provides the comfort and confidence that drive you toward realizing your wildest dreams.

This is truly what life's all about—doing everything we possibly can each day to shift the emphasis toward positivity and steer our world's focus in a better direction moving forward.

FINAL THOUGHTS

Throughout this book, I have taken the opportunity to discuss a different approach to life and a different perspective on this world. I truly feel that we're all in this together, united by a common purpose to make the world a better place. My intent through this process has strictly been to do my part in spreading the message of positivity to as many people as possible. The more we share our natural abilities with those around us, the greater our potential for fulfilling our destinies in life. I would like to summarize my writing and leave you with some thoughts to consider so that you can make the most of this experience.

We are all born with a blank slate and a new beginning. The puzzles of our lives start off empty, without any pieces. However, we are all given the ability to put our puzzles together and make them truly our own. As life progresses, we continually grow and develop, picking up the pieces as we go along. It isn't always easy to find them, but our inner curiosity and persistence guide us along the way. When we look back later in life, with all our pieces in place, we'll be able to fully comprehend our true purpose and reason for being. With this precious gift of life held close in our hands, today's opportunities are here at our fingertips. What we make of such opportunities is strictly up to each and every one of us.

As I discussed from the beginning, the foundation of a positive life is centered on three basic principles— learning, living, and loving. Collectively these principles establish the potential within us all to do something truly special. When used for their intended purpose, they serve as our template for building that puzzle of life. The remainder of this summary includes my personal definitions of these three components and their overall message throughout *The Power of the Positive.*

Learning

Learning is the capacity within each of us to continually evolve and improve.

It now becomes clear that learning has a much deeper meaning than you may have originally thought. Learning requires you to develop an openness and understanding of your inner feelings and emotions. With such awareness, you not only connect with your soul, but also with your surroundings. As you engage in these interactions, make a point to be observant of what's really going on, and refuse to merely see what's on the surface of life. Pride yourself on being a good listener to those who matter most in your life. You will find life much more rewarding by listening more than you speak. In doing so, you'll learn about the intricacies of hidden worlds you never knew existed.

Learning is also about connecting with your true passions and embracing your role in life. Self-reflection provides a means to open these pathways and remove the walls of separation. Create an environment that allows your heart's desires to shine through. Embrace the raw talents you possess, and be a teacher of these abilities to those around you. You will know exactly what these are when you feel how effortless it is to exude them. The passion within will always be there to point you in the right direction.

This deep understanding of your presence in life will invigorate your heart to generate positive visions of your future. These dreams collectively serve as the guiding lights that illuminate your passage through life. Throughout this incredible adventure, learn to absorb the offerings of your surroundings, and give back to the world by simply living your reason for being.

Living

Living is the true and pure essence of our ultimate purpose.

Now that you've established an openness and awareness to the world, you can begin to pursue your calling. You have to realize that your time, your life, your moment is now. Stop waiting for a better tomorrow, and start grasping the opportunity of today. Refuse to see your past as a limit to your ultimate potential. Yesterday is history—learn from it, become better, and move forward. Tomorrow is not here yet—it is a time for opportunities to be discovered later, but there are too many yet to be explored today. Now is the time to start living your true life story and being the great person you know you are. Each new day you are given another opportunity at life, you are presented with a new blank slate, just as you were when you first arrived in this world.

As you put your focus and attention on the present, the key is living your true priorities. Set high expectations for yourself, and work hard to live up to them. Take the time to evaluate whether your actions each day represent those priorities and expectations. Make the most of every chance you get to do something great. Appreciate everything you have been blessed with and all that is good in your life.

Do your best to see every situation from an optimistic point of view. Take a proactive and strong approach to everything you choose to pursue. The positive energy you put out will always find its way back to you. Through life's obstacles, work hard to eliminate sources of negativity and lead by example in doing what's right. Do not allow the opinions or views of others distract you from everything you strive to achieve. Embrace the freedom that comes from living a simple life and removing unnecessary pressures and constraints.

Always know that you truly deserve the best that life has to offer, and never accept anything less. Stay true to yourself in all that you do, and preserve the independence you know and love. Be confident and proud of who you are and everything you represent. Without pride, you are nothing; with it, you are everything. Through living a more positive life, you will learn to cherish the strength, happiness, and fulfillment life can bring.

As life progresses, be flexible and adapt to the changes you will experience both personally and those taking place around you. Develop a state of ease and patience throughout your journey. Some things take more time to develop than others, but always know that everything will fall into place when the time is right. Trust yourself, and allow your emotions to be the drivers of your ambitions in life.

The key to embracing the power of the positive that lies within is being the best you possibly can be every day you live your life. Show the world why you're here, and allow them to feel your emotional connection with the world. Most importantly, give them a true sense of the love that emanates from your soul.

Loving

Loving is the embodiment of the most extreme positive emotion we have the ability to feel.

In a world so vast and complex, there exists one common thread that ties us all together. Love is that universal connection between our hearts. As you become more comfortable with your place in this world, listen to that voice inside your heart for your life purpose. Among all the other opinions and beliefs in this world, demand that your inner voice is heard. Ensure that it serves as your guide, and refuse to allow it to be silenced.

With a positive approach to this world, there's nothing that will get in your way or prevent you from reaching your true potential. When you find yourself dealing with uncertainty, make a point to act on the feelings of your heart and not the thoughts of your mind. As I said before, love is everlasting, and no matter how far we waver off course, it always points us back down our path of destiny.

Learning, living, and loving—embrace their presence in life, and determine what they mean to you.

To put it simply:

Learn from yesterday; live for today; be better for tomorrow.

I hope that after reading this, you now have a different perspective on the world we live in. In no way do I feel that these thoughts and philosophies are the basis by which everyone should live their lives. I have simply taken this opportunity to share my personal views in order to promote a more positive world. I know that as we all progress through life, we will continue to realize our purpose in this place. Personally, I know that I am meant to be here to share this positive outlook with the world and lead by example to show others how they too can live a life of dreams. If you took at least one message from this book that will help you live a better life, I consider that a true success. Now, I simply ask you to clear your mind, open your heart, and take the time to truly evaluate how you view the world and where you fit in this amazing thing called life. In doing so, ask yourself these two final questions:

How do you want to be remembered in this world? What legacy and mark will you leave behind when your life's puzzle is complete?

As you determine your response to these questions, keep in mind that your daily interactions with the world around you directly represent the legacy you ultimately leave. Be an inspiration to those around you and a leader in motivating others to aspire for greatness. If you only have one impression to give, make it special and make it memorable.

Always remember, the power of an individual can change a life, but the power of the positive can change the world.

A MESSAGE FROM THE AUTHOR

Now that you have finished reading this book, I know that you will relate these thoughts and messages to your own life journey. I hope you strongly connected to *The Power of the Positive*'s theme of learning from the experiences of others so that we can all become better and promote a more positive world. I ask that you send notes and personal writings to me via *thepowerofthepositive.com* or *The Power of the Positive*'s Facebook page so that I can learn from your view of the world. I plan on writing my second book about the feedback I receive from each and every one of you. I want to share your story, your ideals, and the power that lies within you.

The power of an individual can change a life, but the power of the positive can change the world.

LaVergne, TN USA
16 February 2011

216666LV00004B/1/P